From Your Friends at The MAILBOX®

Preschool–Kindergarten

I CAN MAKE IT!
I CAN READ IT!

SCIENCE

20 Reproducible Booklets to Develop Early Science & Literacy Skills

Managing Editor: Cindy K. Daoust
Editor at Large: Diane Badden
Contributing Writers: Susan Bunyan, Susan DeRiso, Lucia Kemp Henry, Suzanne Moore
Copy Editors: Sylvan Allen, Karen Brewer Grossman, Karen L. Huffman, Amy Kirtley-Hill, Debbie Shoffner
Cover Artist: Nick Greenwood
Art Coordinator: Cathy Spangler Bruce
Artist: Cathy Spangler Bruce
Contributing Artist: Lucia Kemp Henry
Typesetters: Lynette Dickerson, Mark Rainey

President, The Mailbox Book Company™: Joseph C. Bucci
Director of Book Planning and Development: Chris Poindexter
Book Development Managers: Elizabeth H. Lindsay, Thad McLaurin, Susan Walker
Curriculum Director: Karen P. Shelton
Traffic Manager: Lisa K. Pitts
Librarian: Dorothy C. McKinney
Editorial and Freelance Management: Karen A. Brudnal
Editorial Training: Irving P. Crump
Editorial Assistants: Hope Rodgers, Jan E. Witcher

WITHDRAWN

www.themailbox.com

Manufactured in the United States
10 9 8 7 6 5 4 3 2

TABLE OF CONTENTS

I AM A SCIENTIST

Boost youngsters' scientific self-esteem and reinforce process skills with this booklet about being a scientist. In advance, gather a small photo of each child in your class; then duplicate pages 4–8 to make a class supply. Cut out the opening in the booklet backing on page 8 for each child; then tape each child's picture behind the opening. Distribute page 8 and the remaining pages (pages 4–7) to each child and have her color them as desired. To make the booklet cover, have each student cut out the text box and glue it in the space provided and then write her name on the line. Next, have her cut out each booklet page and matching patterns and then glue the patterns in the appropriate spaces on each page. Help the student sequence the pages behind the cover and then staple them along the left-hand side. Invite student partners to read their booklets to each other. Then have students take their booklets home to share with their families.

EXTENSION ACTIVITY

Ask youngsters to brainstorm a list of other classroom items they can observe, measure, or compare; then record their answers on a chart.

DID YOU KNOW?

- Observation involves using one or more of the five senses to gain information.
- Measurement compares objects to standard units (inches or feet) or nonstandard units (cubes or paper clips).
- Controlling variables (such as withholding water from one plant) affects the outcome of experiments.
- Other science process skills include classifying, predicting, and graphing.

I AM A SCIENTIST

by Sandy

I observe. 1

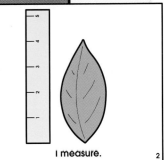

I measure. 2

No Water   Water

I compare. 3

I am a scientist. 4

Booklet Cover and Pattern
Use with "I Am a Scientist" on page 3.

Glue title here.

by

_____

©The Education Center, Inc

I AM A SCIENTIST

Glue hand lens here.

Glue plant here.

I observe.

1

plant

hand lens

Booklet Page and Patterns
Use with "I Am a Scientist" on page 3.

Glue ruler here.

Glue
leaf
here.

I measure.

2

ruler

leaf

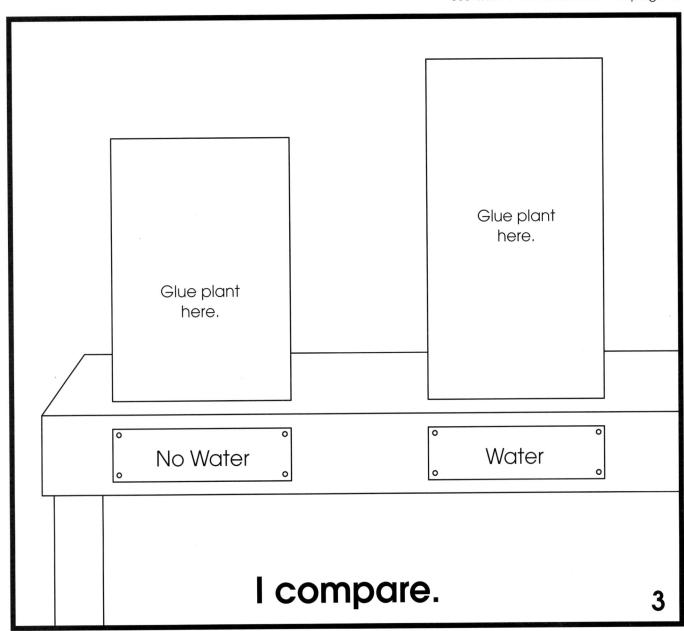

Glue plant here.

Glue plant here.

No Water

Water

I compare.

3

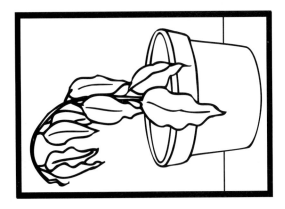

Booklet Backing and Pattern
Use with "I Am a Scientist" on page 3.

Cut out.

Glue plant here.

°How tall will the° plant grow?

I am a scientist.

4

plant

A DUCK'S TALE

Your little ducklings will take to this tale like a duck takes to water as they learn about the life cycle process. In advance, copy pages 10–12 to make a class supply (make enough copies of the wing pattern for each child to have five). Have each child color and cut out the patterns, text boxes, booklet pages, and backing. Help each child follow the directions below to complete each page. Then help her sequence the pages behind the cover and staple them onto the backing. Help each child read her booklet and ask her to tell how the duck changed as it grew. Encourage her to take her booklet home to share with her family.

PAGE-DECORATING INSTRUCTIONS

Cover: Write your name.

Page 1: Glue text box 1 in place on a wing. Attach the two egg halves with a brad.

Page 2: Glue text box 2 in place on a wing. Glue the duckling above the text box and then glue yellow cotton onto the duckling.

Page 3: Glue text box 3 in place on a wing. Glue the duck above the text box and then attach the foot with a brad where indicated.

Page 4: Glue text box 4 in place on a wing. Glue the feather above the text box.

Page 5: Glue text box 5 in place on a wing. Glue the food above the text box.

Backing: Glue paper grass below the egg.

EXTENSION ACTIVITY

Demonstrate for youngsters how a duck's oily feathers give protection. Ask youngsters to observe as you add a few droplets of vegetable oil to a pan of water (*the oil and water do not mix*). Guide youngsters to understand that a duck's oily feathers help keep it dry and warm even when it's swimming in water.

DID YOU KNOW?

- A duck is a water bird that hatches from an egg.
- A duck has oil glands located near its tail that keep its feathers waterproof.
- A duck eats seeds, plants, insects, and small fish that it finds in the water.

A Duck's Tale
by Ashley

My baby feathers were soft and yellow. 2

My feathers are oily to keep me dry. 4

I lay my eggs in soft grass. 6

I hatched from an egg. 1

My feet are webbed to paddle. 3

I eat seeds, insects, plants, and fish. 5

A DUCK'S TALE

by _____

©The Education Center, Inc.

Glue text box here.

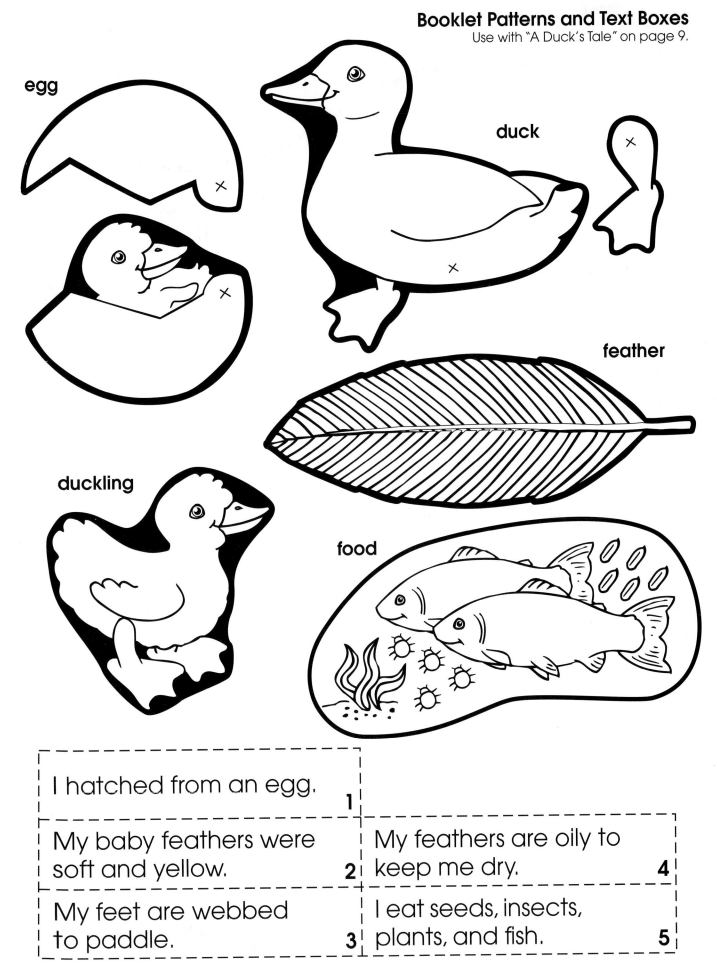

egg

duck

feather

duckling

food

I hatched from an egg.　1

My baby feathers were soft and yellow.　2

My feet are webbed to paddle.　3

My feathers are oily to keep me dry.　4

I eat seeds, insects, plants, and fish.　5

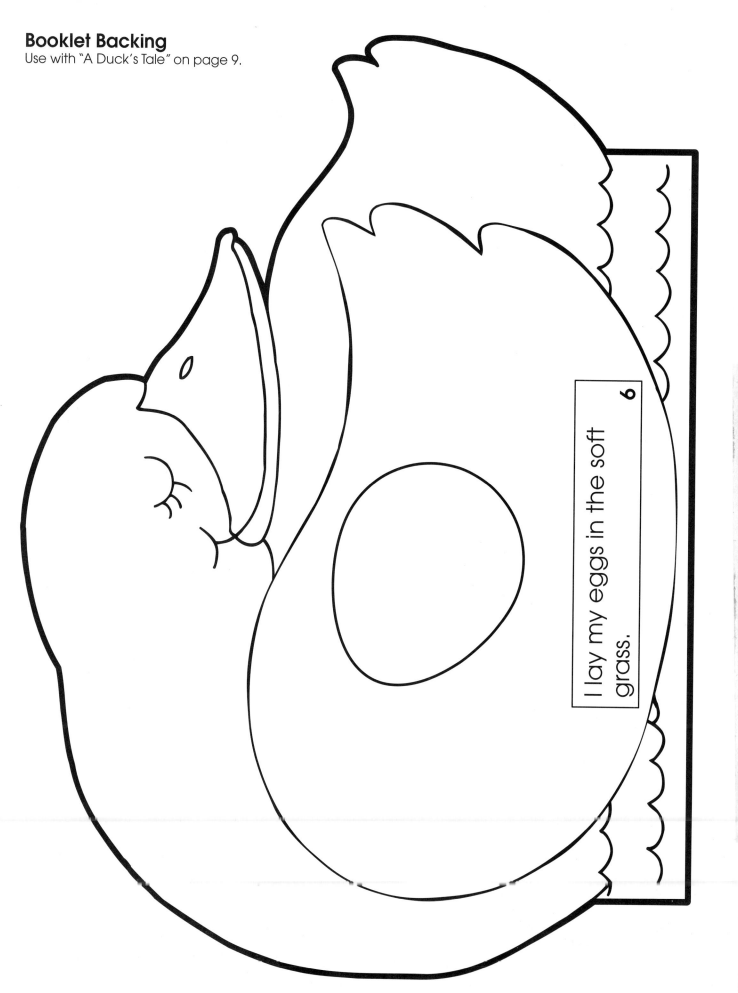

I lay my eggs in the soft grass.

6

WHERE DO I LIVE?

Have your little explorers help each animal find its habitat by reading the clues in this lift-the-flap booklet. To prepare, copy pages 14–17 to make a class supply (make enough copies of the circle pattern on page 15 for each child to have five). Have each child color the cover and animal patterns and then cut out all the pieces. Help each child glue a text box on each booklet page, where indicated, to create a flap. Then sequence the pages behind the cover and staple them together at the top as shown. Help the child read the clue on each booklet page and decide which animal lives in that habitat. Ask her to lift the flap and glue the correct animal pattern underneath as shown. Invite each child to read her booklet to a partner and then take it home to share with her family.

EXTENSION ACTIVITY

Invite youngsters to share their experiences of different animal habitats. Then help them create a class animal-habitat mural on bulletin board paper. Have students illustrate a habitat and then cut out and glue on magazine pictures of animals that live in that environment.

DID YOU KNOW?

- A habitat is where animals live and grow.
- Some animals build a temporary home in their habitat, such as when a bird builds a nest that it uses for a short time.
- Some animals carry their homes with them as they move about within their habitats, such as a hermit crab with a mollusk shell.
- Some animals don't build a home but move about their habitat, such as deer in the forest.
- It is important to treat all animal habitats with respect, such as by not touching a bird's nest because it will harm the bird or its eggs.

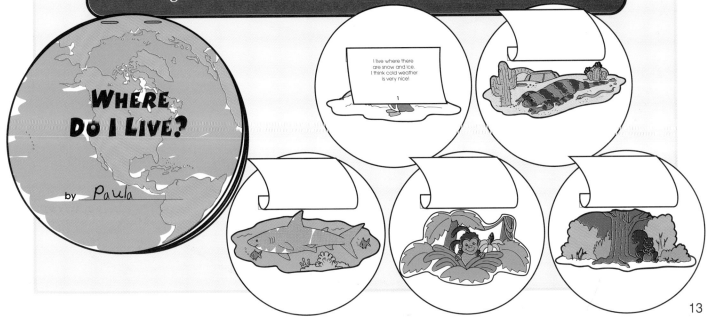

WHERE DO I LIVE?

by Paula

I live where there are snow and ice. I think cold weather is very nice!

1

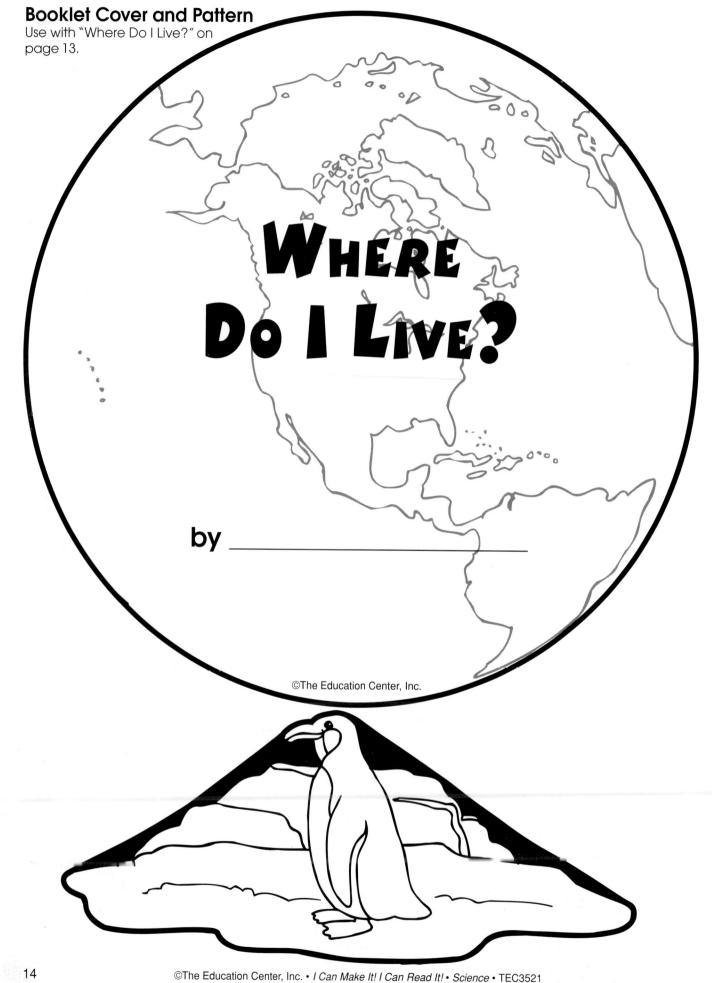

WHERE
DO I LIVE?

by _____

©The Education Center, Inc.

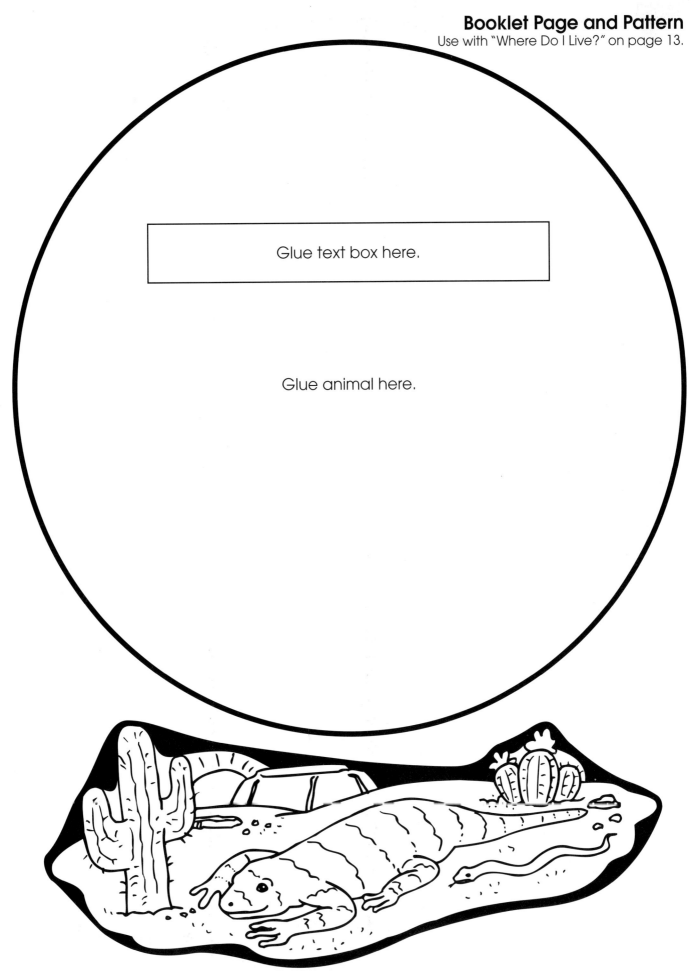

Glue text box here.

Glue animal here.

Booklet Patterns
Use with "Where Do I Live?" on page 13.

I live on very
dry, hot land,
Not many trees
but lots of sand!

2

I live down in the
deep, blue sea.
Lots of water is
home to me!

3

I live in a jungle so
lush and green.
Swinging in high trees
I can be seen!

4

I live where there
are snow and ice.
I think cold weather
is very nice!

1

I live in a forest.
I'm always in a rush,
Eating nuts and berries I find
hidden in the brush!

5

I AM A PUMPKIN!

Harvest reading and writing skills as youngsters create this pumpkin life cycle booklet. To begin, copy pages 19–21 to make a class supply and gather two six-inch paper plates for each child. You will also need paint, glue, crayons, paint sponges, pumpkin seeds, cotton swabs, green yarn, orange tissue paper, and green construction paper available for each child to use. Instruct each child to sponge-paint one side of each paper plate. When the paint is dry, help her write the booklet title on the painted side of each plate. Then have her glue a two-inch green construction paper stem onto the back of one plate as shown. Have her cut out the booklet pages and then follow the directions below to complete each page. Then help her sequence the pages, place them between the painted plates, and staple the booklet together along the left side as shown. Invite each child to take her booklet home to share her pumpkin growth knowledge with her family.

PAGE-DECORATING INSTRUCTIONS

Page 1: Glue on a pumpkin seed and color ground around it.

Page 2: Color the sun yellow. Use a cotton swab to paint on blue raindrops.

Page 3: Color the ground brown. Press a green paint fingerprint sprout onto the ground.

Page 4: Color the ground brown. Glue on a piece of green yarn to represent the vine.

Page 5: Color the ground brown and the vine green. Glue on a piece of orange tissue paper to represent the pumpkin flower.

Page 6: Color the ground brown and the vine green. Glue on a one-inch green construction paper circle to represent the growing pumpkin.

EXTENSION ACTIVITY

Help each child plant a pumpkin seed in a cup of soil. When the seeds have sprouted, send them home for outdoor planting.

DID YOU KNOW?

- Pumpkins belong to the gourd family.
- It takes about 120 days for a pumpkin to grow.
- Pollen from a male pumpkin flower must pollinate a female pumpkin flower for growth.
- Bees and other insects help pollinate pumpkin flowers.

I Am a Pumpkin by Kalen

1. I am a tiny pumpkin seed.
2. Water and sun are what I need.
3. Watch me sprout out of the ground.
4. See my vine grow all around.
5. Soon a flower will be seen.
6. Then my fruit, a ball of green.

I am a tiny pumpkin seed.

1

Water and sun are what I need.

2

Watch me sprout out of the ground.

3

See my vine grow all around.

4

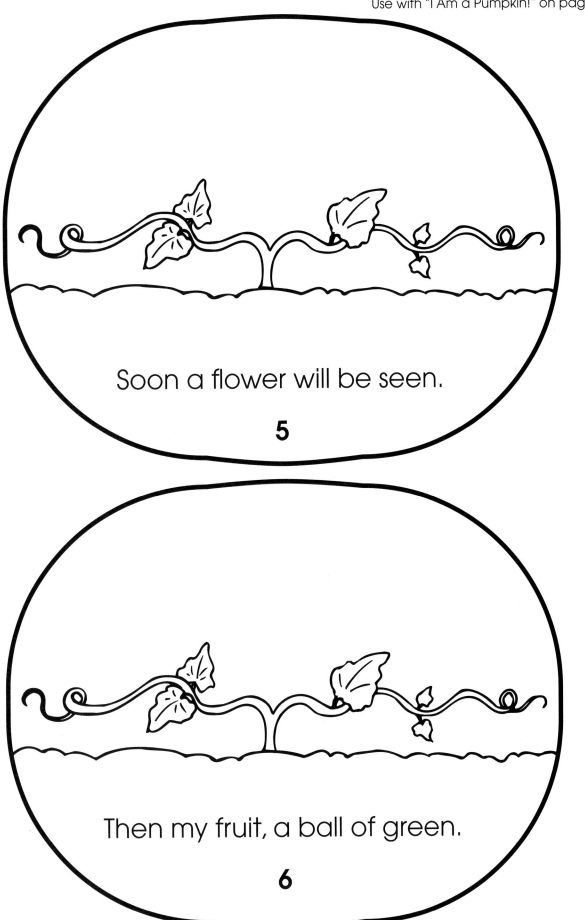

Soon a flower will be seen.

5

Then my fruit, a ball of green.

6

SURPRISE!

This fruity booklet will grow on youngsters as they learn about the life cycle of a watermelon. To prepare, copy pages 23–25 to make a class supply. You will also need several watermelon seeds for each child (or substitute black thumbprints to represent seeds). Have each child cut out the booklet pages and then follow the directions below to complete each page. Then have him sequence the pages behind the cover and staple them together along the left side. Encourage him to read his booklet and then take it home to share with his family.

PAGE-DECORATING INSTRUCTIONS

Cover: Color the vines and then write your name.

Page 1: Color the seed packet. Glue several seeds below the packet (or make several black thumbprints).

Page 2: Color the page and then glue one seed on the hand and several seeds underground.

Page 3: Color. If desired, trace the water sprinkle with a blue glitter crayon. Glue several seeds underground.

Page 4: Color. Press two green fingerprints on top of each stem to represent sprouting seeds.

Page 5: Color. If desired, brush green paint over the entire watermelon and let dry.

EXTENSION ACTIVITY

Cut open a real watermelon and have youngsters observe and save the seeds. Then have each child plant a few seeds in a soil-filled cup and place the cup in a sunny window. Keep the soil moist and in approximately a week watch for watermelon sprouts.

DID YOU KNOW?
- Seeds come in different shapes, sizes, and colors.
- All seeds have a baby plant inside of them.
- All seeds have some food inside to help the baby plant grow after the seed is planted.
- All seeds have a seed coat, or covering, to protect the baby seed.

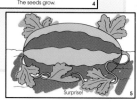

Surprise!

by

_____

©The Education Center, Inc.

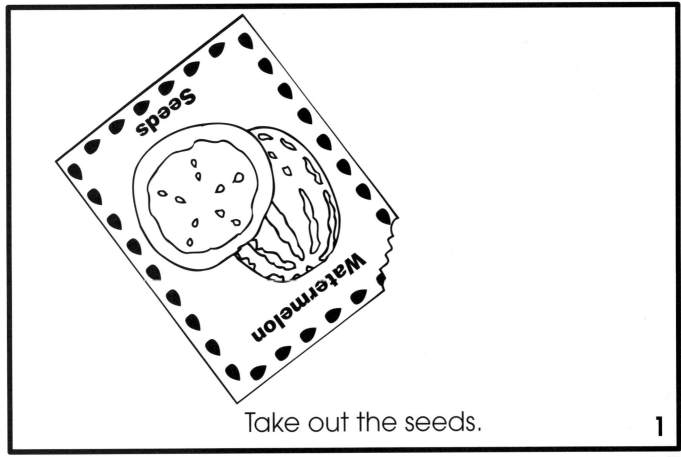

Take out the seeds.

1

Plant the seeds.

2

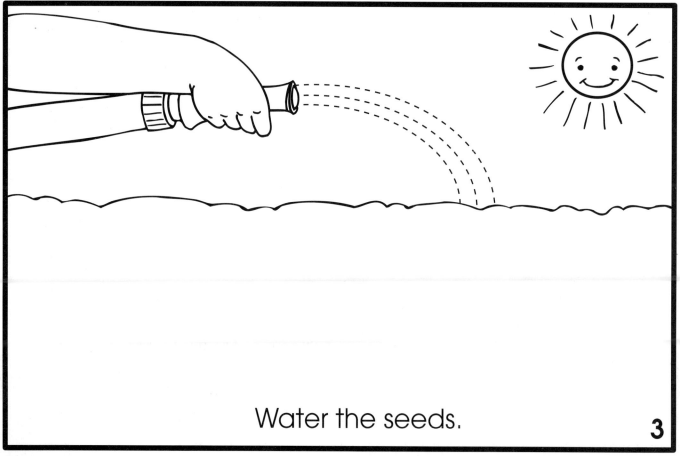

Water the seeds.

3

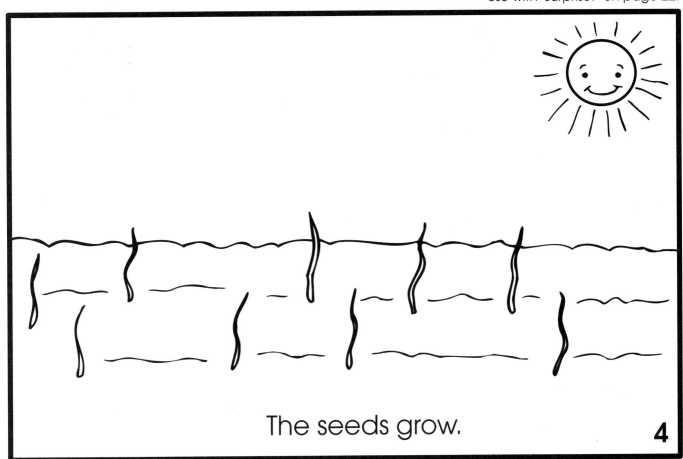

The seeds grow.

4

Surprise!

5

LOOK AT ME—I'M A BEE!

Youngsters will get the buzz on insect parts with this easy-as-can-be booklet! To begin, copy pages 27–30 on yellow construction paper to make a class supply. Have each child cut out the booklet pages and follow the directions below to complete each page. Afterward, help her glue the pages together where indicated and then accordion-fold the booklet as shown. Invite her to read her booklet and then take it home to share with family.

PAGE-DECORATING INSTRUCTIONS

Cover: Write your name. Color the wings white.

Page 1: Glue on two wiggle eyes.

Page 2: Curl each top of two two-inch black pipe cleaners to represent antennae and then glue them onto the page.

Page 3: Glue on six two-inch thin black construction paper strips to represent legs.

Page 4: Glue on two two-inch diameter white tissue paper circles to represent wings.

Page 5: Use a cotton swab to paint on six black stripes.

Page 6: Glue on a toothpick to represent a stinger.

Page 7: Color the wings white.

EXTENSION ACTIVITY

Offer youngsters a sweet honey treat! Simply whip butter and honey together and spread it on graham crackers. It's "un-bee-lievably" good!

DID YOU KNOW?

- Insects have three body parts: the head, the thorax, and the abdomen.
- Insects have antennae and three pairs of legs.
- Insects usually have wings.
- Many bees have stingers, but the honeybee dies after stinging.
- Adult bees only eat nectar and honey.

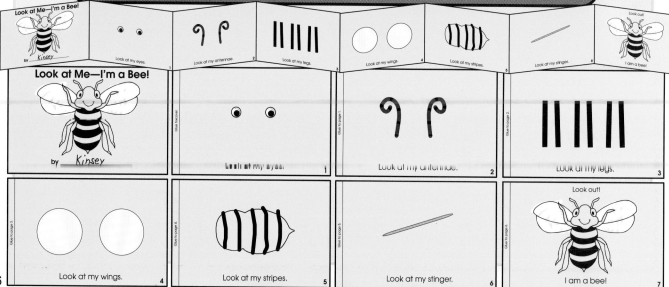

26

Look at Me—I'm a Bee!

by _____

Glue to cover.

Look at my eyes.

1

Glue to page 1.

Look at my antennae.

2

Glue to page 2.

Look at my legs.

3

Glue to page 3.

Look at my wings.

4

Glue to page 4.

Look at my stripes.

5

Glue to page 5.

Look at my stinger.

6

Glue to page 6.

Look out!

I am a bee!

7

THE CATERPILLAR

Your little butterflies will flutter around this caterpillar life cycle booklet. To prepare, copy pages 32–35 to make a class supply. Ask each child to color and cut out the patterns and booklet pages and then follow the directions below to complete each page. Then help him sequence the pages behind the cover and staple them together along the left side. Invite each child to retell the life cycle of the caterpillar by reading his booklet to a friend.

PAGE-DECORATING INSTRUCTIONS

Cover: Glue the two leaves in place. Glue on two wiggle eyes and two tiny pom-pom antennae.

Page 1: Glue the caterpillar and egg on the leaf.

Page 2: Glue the small caterpillar on the leaf.

Page 3: Glue the large caterpillar on the leaf.

Page 4: Glue the pupa on the stick.

Page 5: Glue the butterfly body in the middle of the wings.

EXTENSION ACTIVITY

Create a set of life cycle sequencing cards for center time. First, mask out the page numbers on a copy of the booklet pages and then complete each page as directed. If desired, laminate the pages for durability.

DID YOU KNOW?

- A female butterfly lays many tiny eggs on a plant leaf.
- When a caterpillar emerges from its egg, it begins to eat the leaf it hatched on.
- Caterpillars eat constantly and grow quickly.
- After the caterpillar surrounds itself in a cocoon (the pupa stage of the life cycle), it begins to change into a butterfly.

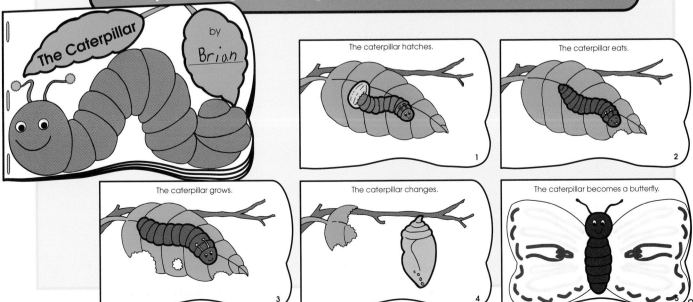

The Caterpillar by Brian

The caterpillar hatches. 1

The caterpillar eats. 2

The caterpillar grows. 3

The caterpillar changes. 4

The caterpillar becomes a butterfly.

Booklet Cover and Page

Use with "The Caterpillar" on page 31.

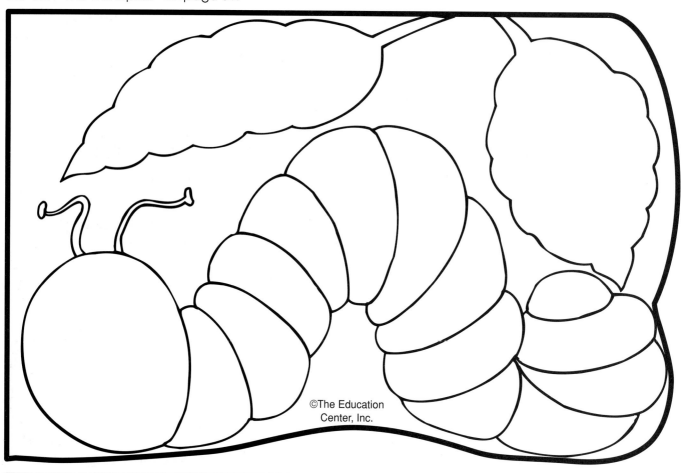

©The Education
Center, Inc.

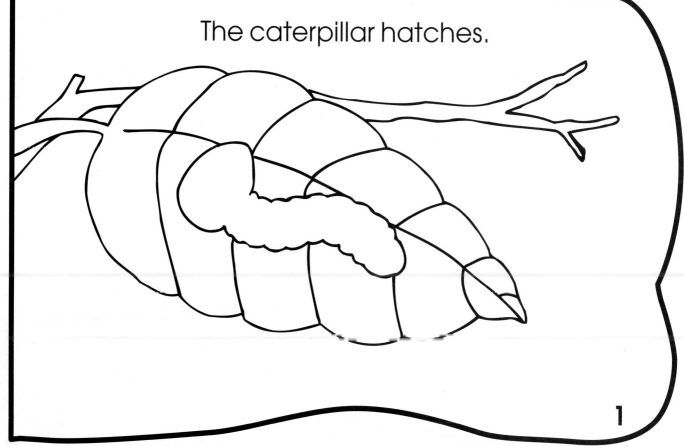

The caterpillar hatches.

1

The caterpillar eats.

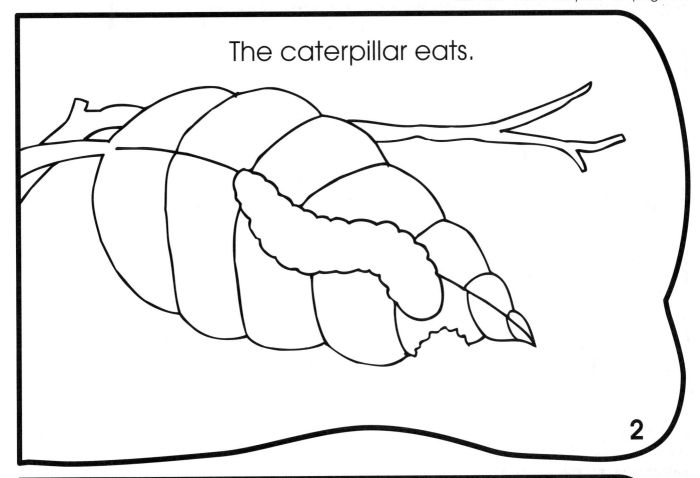

2

The caterpillar grows.

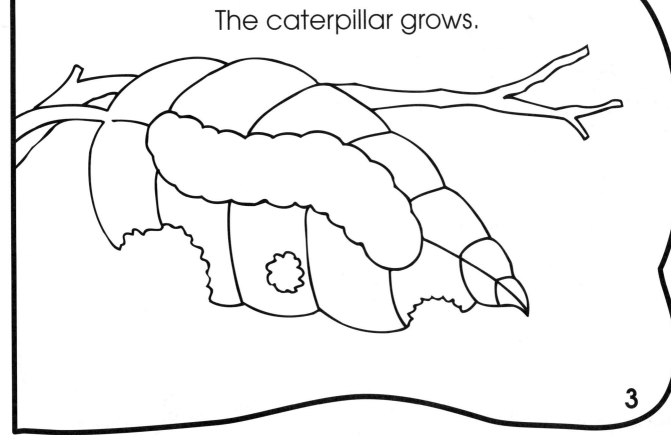

3

The caterpillar changes.

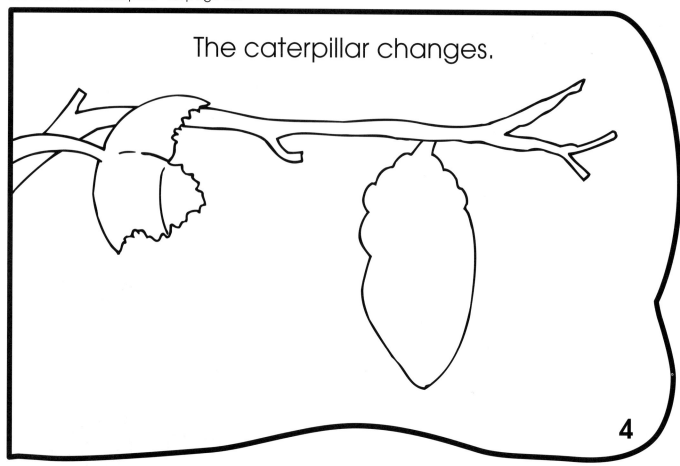

4

The caterpillar becomes a butterfly.

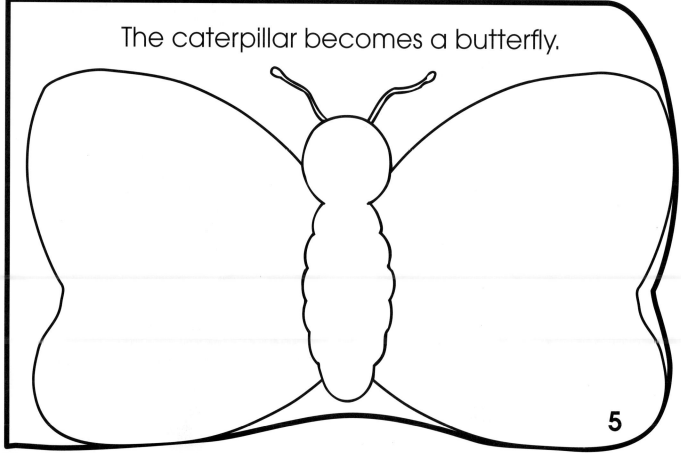

5

leaf

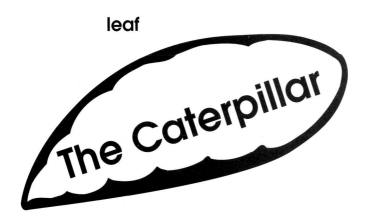

leaf

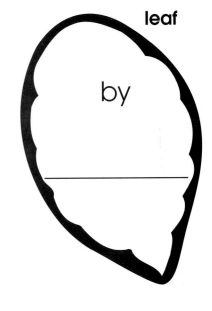

by

caterpillar and egg

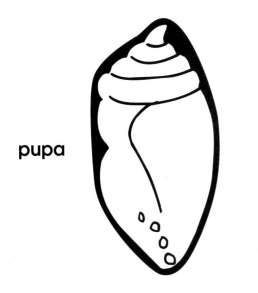

small caterpillar

large caterpillar

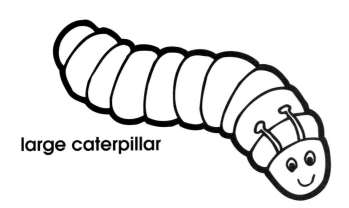

pupa

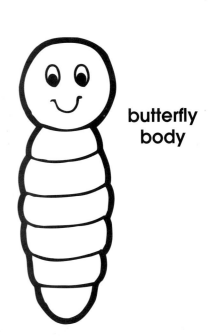

butterfly body

FOUR SEASONS TREE

Summer, fall, winter, spring—to teach youngsters about the four seasons, an apple tree is the thing! In advance, copy pages 37–40 to make a class supply and then cut out the window on each copy of page 39. Have each child color and cut out all the pieces and trace the words on the booklet backing. To assemble a booklet, align the picture wheel behind the backing page so that a picture shows through the window and then use a brad to attach it. Next, sequence the booklet pages behind the cover and staple them onto the backing as shown. Ask each child to follow along in her booklet and turn the picture wheel to the appropriate scene as you read the text. Have her circle her favorite season on the backing. Then invite partners to read booklets together.

EXTENSION ACTIVITY

Have youngsters help make a seasonal apple tree display. Cut four large tree shapes from brown bulletin board paper. Divide students into three groups and give each group one cutout. Ask each group to use construction paper to decorate its tree for one season (spring with pink blossoms, summer with small green apples, and fall with big red apples). Display the trees in seasonal order along with a brown tree trunk to represent winter.

DID YOU KNOW?
- An apple is a fruit that contains seeds needed to grow new trees.
- Spring apple blossoms begin to grow into apples when the petals fall off.
- Summer green apples continue to grow and ripen all season.
- Fall apples are ripe and ready to pick.
- Winter brings a time of rest for the apple tree.

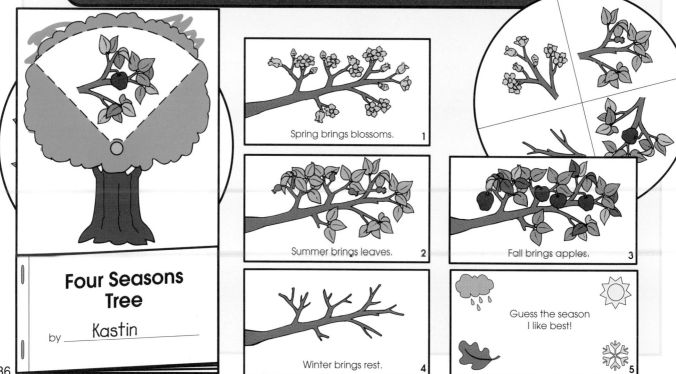

Four Seasons Tree

by Kastin

Spring brings blossoms. 1

Summer brings leaves. 2

Fall brings apples. 3

Winter brings rest. 4

Guess the season I like best! 5

Four Seasons Tree

by _____

Spring brings blossoms.

1

Summer brings leaves.

2

Booklet Pages

Use with "Four Seasons Tree" on page 36.

Fall brings apples.

3

Winter brings rest.

4

Guess the season
I like best!

5

spring
summer
fall
winter

Booklet Wheel

Use with "Four Seasons Tree" on page 36.

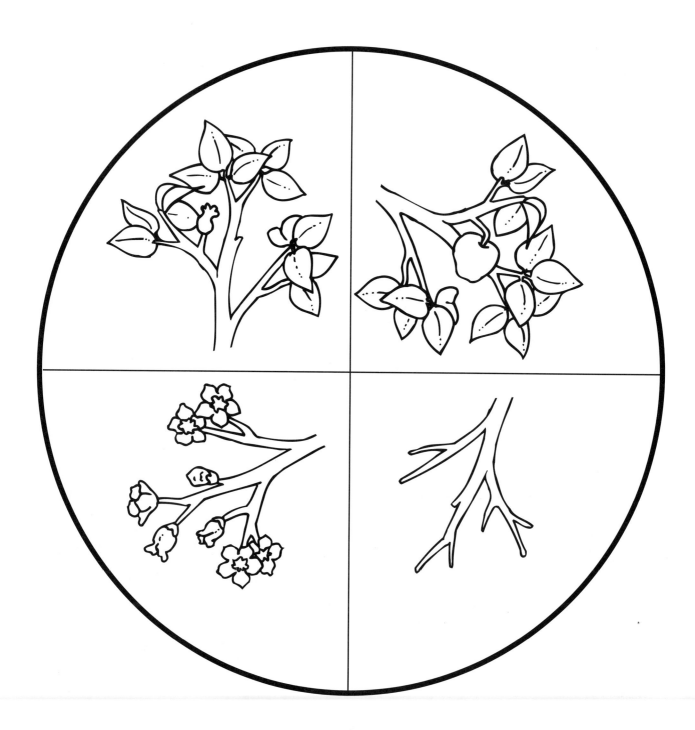

WHAT'S THE WEATHER?

Whether it is sunny, rainy, or snowy, your little weather watchers will enjoy making this picture-perfect booklet. In advance, gather a small photo of each child in your class; then copy pages 42–44 to make a class supply. Cut out the opening on the cover and each booklet page for each child. Then tape each child's photo behind the opening on her copy of booklet page 5. Have each child cut out her booklet pages and then follow the directions below to complete each page. Then help her sequence the pages behind the cover and staple them together along the left side. Invite pairs of youngsters to read each other's booklet. Then have students take their booklets home to share their picture-perfect weather reports.

PAGE-DECORATING INSTRUCTIONS

Cover: Color and write your name.

Page 1: Color and use a blue glitter crayon to trace the raindrops.

Page 2: Use a silver crayon to draw snowflakes and then color the page. Glue a small white pom-pom on each mitten to represent snowballs.

Page 3: Draw a hat and a sun. Color the page.

Page 4: Draw a bird flying. Color the page.

Page 5: Write a word that describes the weather today. Draw clothing and items (for example, sunglasses, sun, and a water sprinkler) that are appropriate for the weather today.

EXTENSION ACTIVITY

Help youngsters create a class graph of their favorite types of weather.

DID YOU KNOW?

- Weather is the way air changes. It can be clear, cloudy, stormy, hot, cold, wet, or dry.
- Weather is the way water in the air changes. Water is the reason there are clouds, rain, snow, and fog.
- Weather can be different during the year, depending on the season. Some areas of the world have just two seasons (wet or dry weather) and some areas have four seasons.
- Weather affects many of our activities and the clothes we wear.

I AM A CLOUD

Youngsters will be on cloud nine as they soar through the cloud types in this booklet. In advance, gather a small photo of each child in your class. You will also need glitter, glue, crayons, cotton balls, aluminum foil, white tissue paper, a white feather, cotton swabs, and blue paint available for each child to use. Copy page 46 on white paper and copy pages 47–49 on light blue paper to make a class supply. Cut out the opening on each page for each child; then tape each child's picture behind the opening on booklet page 6. Ask each child to cut out his booklet pages and then follow the directions below to complete each page. When all the pages are dry, help each child sequence them behind the cover and staple them together along the top as shown. Ask him to follow along in his booklet as you read the text out loud. Encourage him to take his booklet home to share with his family.

PAGE-DECORATING INSTRUCTIONS

Cover: Write your name.

Page 1: Apply glue over the page and then sprinkle it with silver glitter.

Page 2: Glue on two cotton balls that have been pulled into cloud shapes.

Page 3: Glue on a curly white feather.

Page 4: Color the cloud gray and black. Glue on thin strips of aluminum foil twisted into lightning bolt shapes.

Page 5: Color the cloud gray. Glue on thin strips of white tissue paper.

Page 6: Use a cotton swab to dab on blue paint to represent raindrops.

EXTENSION ACTIVITY

For more cloudy information, read *The Cloud Book* by Tomie DePaola to youngsters.

DID YOU KNOW?

- Clouds are suspended ice or water particles.
- Clouds form by the cooling of air that contains water vapor.
- Clouds that form at ground level are called fog.
- Clouds are classified by their height in the sky and their shape.

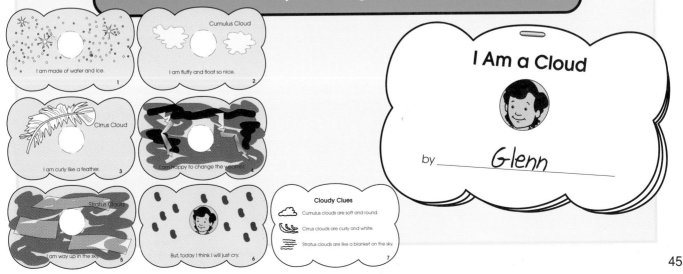

45

I Am a Cloud

Cut out.

by _____

Cloudy Clues

 Cumulus clouds are soft and round.

 Cirrus clouds are curly and white.

 Stratus clouds are like a blanket on the sky.

7

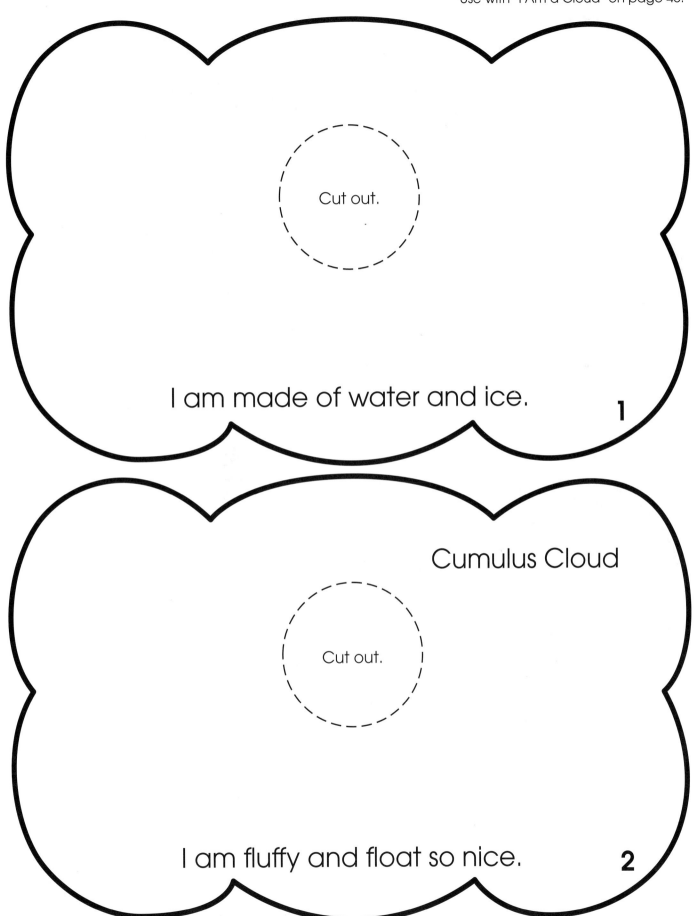

Cut out.

I am made of water and ice.   1

Cumulus Cloud

Cut out.

I am fluffy and float so nice.   2

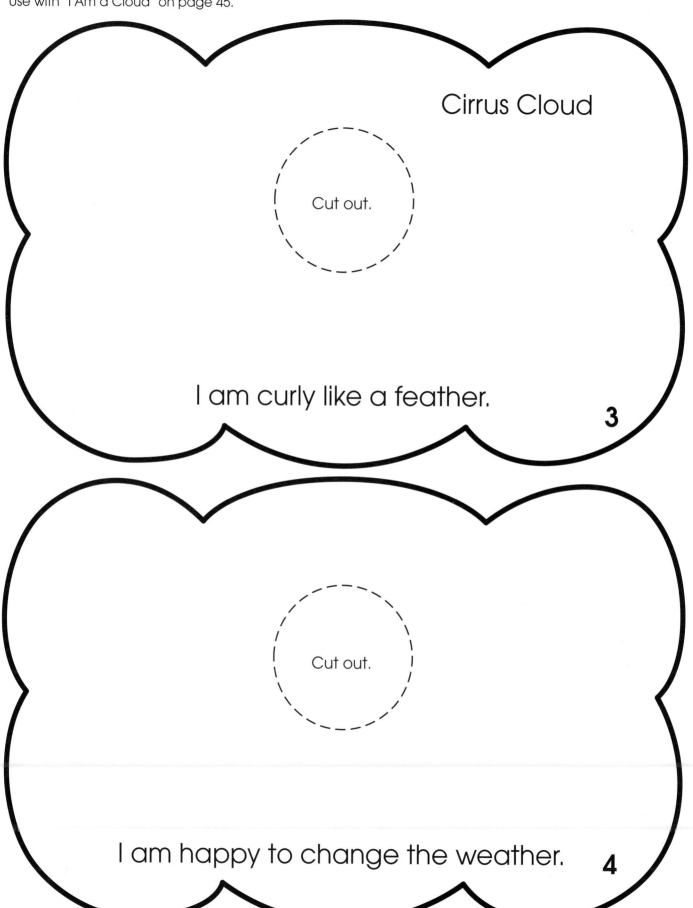

Cirrus Cloud

Cut out.

I am curly like a feather.

3

Cut out.

I am happy to change the weather.

4

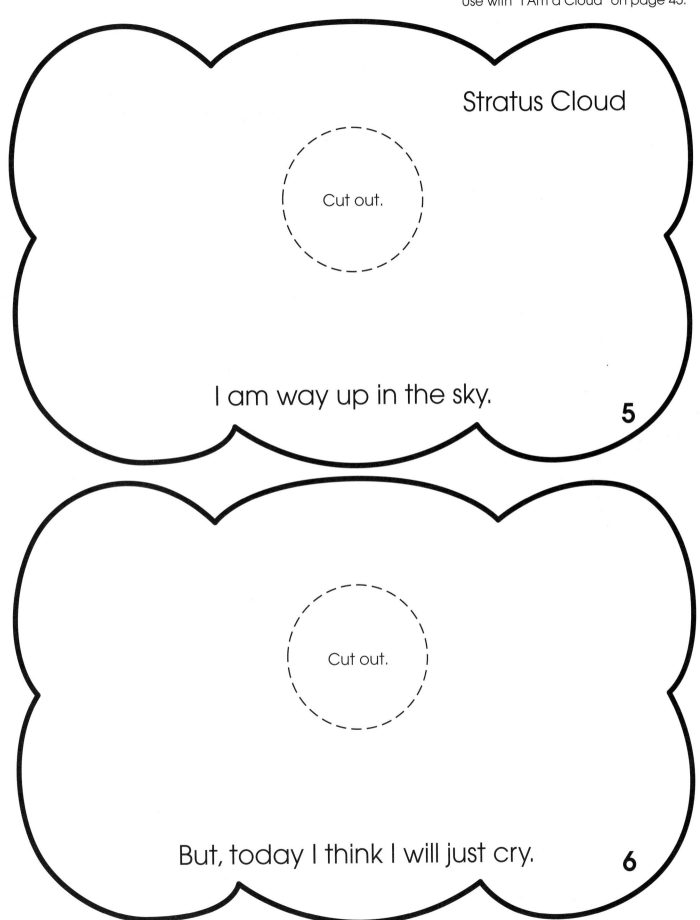

Stratus Cloud

Cut out.

I am way up in the sky.

5

Cut out.

But, today I think I will just cry.

6

SOCKS AND SHOES

Pull on the perfect pair as youngsters practice comparing and describing with this double-sided booklet. In advance, set up a rubbings center by taping a variety of textured flat materials onto a table (such as plastic craft canvas and sandpaper). Copy pages 51–54 to make a class supply. You will also need glitter crayons, regular crayons, sequins, white cotton, colored cotton, string, regular glue, and colored glue available for each child to use. Then help each child follow the directions below to complete each booklet page. Have her cut out and sort the pages into two sets (socks and shoes). Help her sequence each set behind its corresponding cover and staple each set onto the backing page as shown. Encourage each child to read her booklet to a partner and then take it home to share with her family.

PAGE-DECORATING INSTRUCTIONS

Cover: Make a colored texture rubbing on the socks and the shoes. Poke two holes in the shoes, thread a string, and tie it into a bow. Write your name on the blank.

Page 1: Make a different colored texture rubbing on the socks and the shoes.

Page 2: Color the socks in a two-color pattern. Color the shoes with three different colors.

Page 3: Make a colored texture rubbing on the socks and then glue on sequins. Color the shoes with a glitter crayon.

Page 4: Color the socks and shoes.

Page 5: Make a texture rubbing on the socks. Spread colored glue on the boots.

Page 6: Glue white cotton onto the socks. Glue colored cotton onto the slippers.

Backing Page: Draw and color your favorite socks and shoes.

EXTENSION ACTIVITY

Have youngsters observe each other's socks and shoes. Then help them sort the group by sock color and then by shoe style.

DID YOU KNOW?

- We can describe objects, like socks and shoes, by their physical properties.
- We use our senses (sight, touch, smell, taste, hearing) to identify physical properties.
- Some physical properties include size, shape, texture, and color.

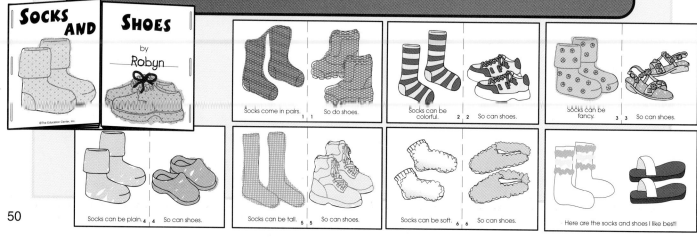

Socks come in pairs. 1 | 1 So do shoes.

Socks can be colorful. 2 | 2 So can shoes.

Socks can be fancy. 3 | 3 So can shoes.

Socks can be plain. 4 | 4 So can shoes.

Socks can be tall. 5 | 5 So can shoes.

Socks can be soft. 6 | 6 So can shoes.

Here are the socks and shoes I like best!

Socks and Shoes

Shoes

by

_____

Socks come in pairs.

1

1

So do shoes.

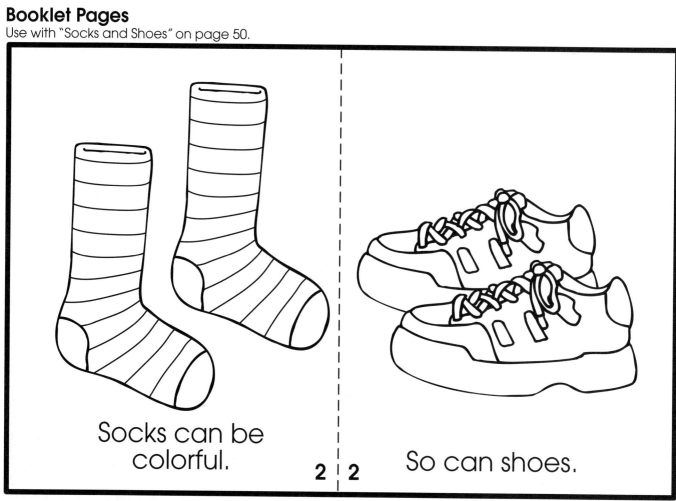

Socks can be colorful.

2 | 2

So can shoes.

Socks can be fancy.

3 | 3

So can shoes.

Socks can be plain. **4** **4** So can shoes.

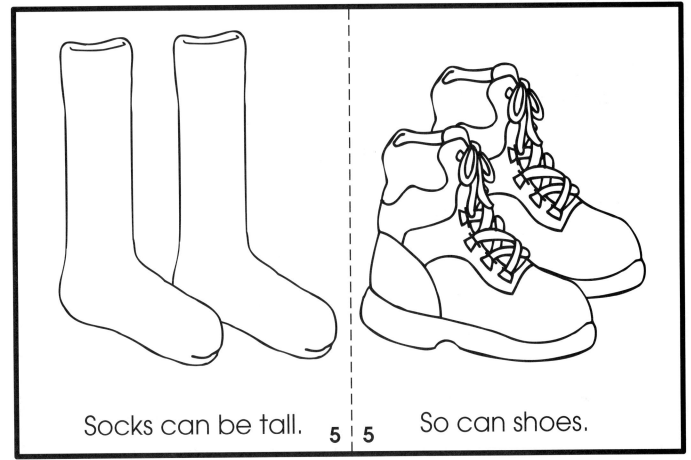

Socks can be tall. **5** **5** So can shoes.

Booklet Pages and Backing Page

Use with "Socks and Shoes" on page 50.

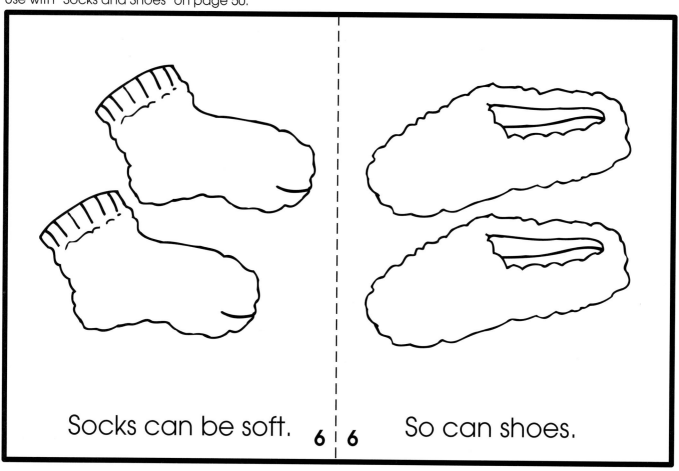

Socks can be soft. 6 | 6 So can shoes.

Here are the socks and shoes I like best!

BEAR'S ADVENTURE

In this sweet booklet, Bear takes youngsters on a sensory adventure in which he uses everything but his common sense. To begin, copy pages 56–59 to make a class supply. (Make enough copies of page 58 for each child to have five.) Read the poem to youngsters. Ask each child to color and cut out his pages and patterns. Then have him follow the directions below to complete each page. Afterward, have him sequence the pages behind the cover and staple them together along the left side. Encourage him to take his booklet home and ask a family member to read the poem out loud before he reads the text.

PAGE-DECORATING INSTRUCTIONS

Cover: Write your name. Glue Bear's head on the right side of the hive as shown.

Page 1: Write "1" at the bottom of the booklet poem page.

Page 2: Write "2" at the bottom. Glue the word *hear* in the space provided. Glue the bee pattern above the sentence.

Page 3: Write "3" at the bottom. Glue the word *smell* in the space provided. Glue the honeycomb pattern above the sentence.

Page 4: Write "4" at the bottom. Glue the word *see* in the space provided. Glue the hive pattern above the sentence.

Page 5: Write "5" at the bottom. Glue the word *taste* in the space provided. Glue the eating-bear pattern above the sentence.

Page 6: Write "6" at the bottom. Glue the word *feel* in the space provided. Glue the bear-and-bees pattern above the sentence.

EXTENSION ACTIVITY

Extend this activity with a sweet edible experiment. Give each child a cracker with honey spread on it. As he nibbles the treat, ask him to think about all the senses he is using (*hearing the crunches, smelling the honey, seeing the cracker and honey, feeling the sticky honey and rough cracker, tasting sweet and salty*).

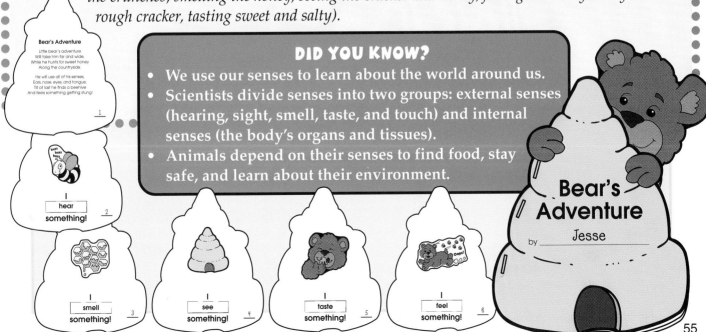

Bear's Adventure

Little bear's adventure
Will take him far and wide,
While he hunts for sweet honey
Along the countryside.

He will use all of his senses,
Ears, nose, eyes, and tongue,
Till at last he finds a beehive
And feels something getting stung!

1

I **hear** something! 2

DID YOU KNOW?

- We use our senses to learn about the world around us.
- Scientists divide senses into two groups: external senses (hearing, sight, smell, taste, and touch) and internal senses (the body's organs and tissues).
- Animals depend on their senses to find food, stay safe, and learn about their environment.

I **smell** something! 3

I **see** something! 4

I **taste** something! 5

I **feel** something! 6

Bear's Adventure
by Jesse

55

Bear's
Adventure

by _____

Bear's Adventure

Little bear's adventure
Will take him far and wide,
While he hunts for sweet honey
Along the countryside.

He will use all of his senses,
Ears, nose, eyes, and tongue,
Till at last he finds a beehive
And feels something getting stung!

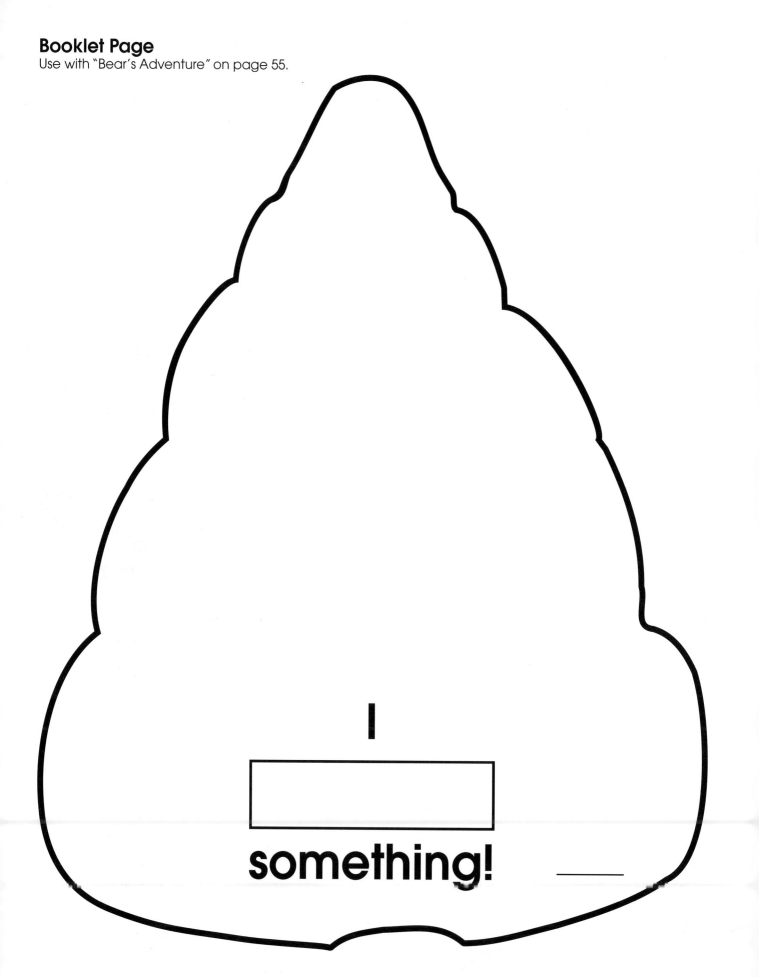

I

something! ____

buzz
buzz
buzz

bee

honeycomb

hive

eating bear

bear and bees

Oops!

text boxes

hear

smell

see

taste

feel

bear's head

Glue behind hive.

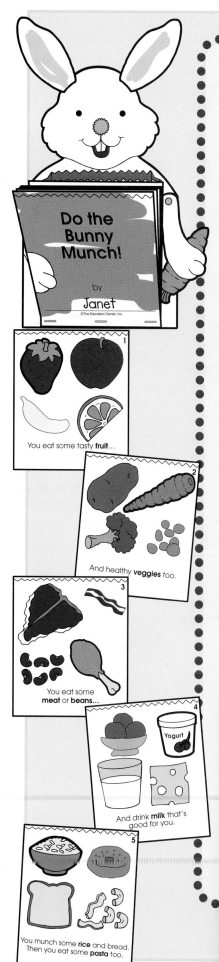

You eat some tasty **fruit**...

And healthy **veggies** too.

You eat some
meat or **beans**...

And drink **milk** that's
good for you.

You munch some **rice** and bread.
Then you eat some **pasta** too.

DO THE BUNNY MUNCH!

Hippity hop! When your little nutritionists create this good food guide, their healthy eating habits will be "munch" improved! In advance, collect several grocery store advertisements and copy pages 61–64 to make a class supply. To introduce the booklet, sing the text on each page to the tune of "The Hokey-Pokey." Then invite youngsters to sing along as you review the text together. Ask each child to color and cut out the booklet pages and patterns. Have her glue each pattern to the appropriate booklet page. Ask each child to draw a different food on each corresponding booklet page. Have her cut out five pictures (one from each food group) from a grocery store advertisement and glue them onto the booklet backing. Help her attach the bunny's arm with a brad and glue on the ears and a pom-pom nose. Then help her sequence the pages behind the cover and staple them onto the booklet backing as shown. Invite each child to take her booklet home to teach her family to "Do the Bunny Munch!"

EXTENSION ACTIVITY

Divide youngsters into five groups and assign each one a different food group. Give each group one paper grocery bag and ask the students to label it accordingly. Ask each group member to draw and color her favorite food from the assigned food group on white paper. Have each child cut out her picture and glue it onto the paper bag. Display the completed bags on a bulletin board titled "Shopping for Healthy Foods."

DID YOU KNOW?

- Vegetables are good sources of fiber, iron, calcium, and vitamins A, B, and C.
- Fruits provide fiber and are a good source of vitamin C. Fruits are a good alternative to sugary snacks.
- Dairy products are good sources of calcium and provide protein and vitamin A.
- Meats, poultry, fish, dried beans and peas, nuts, and eggs are good sources of protein.
- Bread, cereals, and pasta are all made from grain. Foods in this group are a good source of carbohydrates, which provide energy.

1

You eat some tasty **fruit**...

Do the
Bunny
Munch!

by

©The Education Center, Inc.

Booklet Pages and Patterns
Use with "Do the Bunny Munch!" on page 60.

3

You eat some **meat** or **beans**...

2

And healthy **veggies** too.

5

You munch some **rice** and **bread.**
Then you eat some **pasta** too.

4

And drink **milk** that's
good for you.

6

That's what it's all about!

A
Clean
Scene

by
Shandi

1

Whoo needs clean **air?**

2

Whoo needs
clean **water?**

3

Whoo needs
clean **land?**

4

We do—

5

that's
who!

A CLEAN SCENE

Invite youngsters to create this scenic fold-out booklet to highlight our need for clean natural resources. In advance, gather a small photo of each child in your class. Then make a class supply of pages 66–68 and cut a 24-inch length of yarn for each student. Cut out the opening on each copy of booklet page 4; then tape each child's picture behind the opening. Ask each child to color and cut out the booklet pages and patterns. To make the booklet cover, staple the pocket in place with one end of the yarn inside it. Fold the owl pattern along the line and glue the other end of the yarn inside the fold as shown. Then have the child glue each pattern to the appropriate page. Glue the pages together where indicated. Help each child accordion-fold her booklet and then read it as she flies the owl onto each page. Then have her store the owl in the pocket on the cover and take the booklet home to share with her family.

EXTENSION ACTIVITY

Help each child fold a sheet of white paper into thirds. Ask her to color the top section light blue, the middle section dark blue, and the bottom section green. Then have her cut out magazine pictures of air, water, and land animals and glue them to the appropriate sections of the page.

DID YOU KNOW?

- Automobiles and factories emit chemical pollutants that affect our air, water, and land.
- Some chemical pollutants turn to acid in the air and then fall back to the earth in the form of acid rain.
- Acid rain is a form of pollution that can kill trees and make lakes dangerous for fish and other water creatures.
- Pollution can be reduced by using cleaner-burning fuels, such as gas, instead of coal.

GLUE

A Clean Scene

by

_____

©The Education Center, Inc.

1

Whoo needs clean **air?**

Glue page 2 here.

owl

pocket

bird

2

Whoo needs
clean **water?**

fish

3

Whoo needs
clean **land?**

Glue page 4 here.

flower

4

We do—

5

that's
who!

"DINO-MITE" ROCKS!

Youngsters will dig the rocks they find in this booklet! To begin, copy pages 70–74 on white construction paper to make a class supply. You will also need a supply of aluminum foil, watercolors, blue paint, sandpaper, salt, clay, and aquarium gravel. Ask each child to color the dinosaur on each booklet page. Have him follow the directions below to complete each page. Then have him cut out the booklet pages and booklet flaps. Help him glue each rock flap to the corresponding rock creation as shown. Then have him sequence the pages behind the cover and staple them together along the left side. Encourage him to read his booklet to a partner.

PAGE-DECORATING INSTRUCTIONS

Cover: Glue on torn pieces of black, brown, and gray construction paper to represent rocks. Write your name.

Page 1: Color the rock black. Glue on pieces of aluminum foil to represent coal. Let dry.

Page 2: Paint a mixture of glue and blue paint on the rock to represent slate. Let dry.

Page 3: Glue a circle of sandpaper onto the rock to represent sandstone.

Page 4: Apply a layer of glue to the rock and sprinkle on salt to represent quartzite. Let dry.

Page 5: Glue a flattened ball of clay onto the rock to represent clay. Let dry.

Page 6: Paint the rock with watercolors to represent marble. Let dry.

Page 7: Glue aquarium gravel around the dinosaur. Let dry.

EXTENSION ACTIVITY

Invite youngsters to examine a sample of each type of rock that is in their booklets.

DID YOU KNOW?

- Rock makes up the earth's crust.
- Igneous rock is made from hardened molten magma (lava).
- Sedimentary rock is made from particles of sediments (sand, mud, pebbles).
- Metamorphic rock is changed rock. It has been affected by heat and pressure.

"Dino-mite" Rocks!

by

_____

©The Education Center, Inc.

Rocks can be shiny.

1

Rocks can be smooth.

2

Rocks can be rough.

3

Rocks can be hard.

4

Rocks can be soft.

5

Rocks can be colorful.

6

I think rocks are wonderful!

7

Booklet Flaps
Use with "'Dino-mite' Rocks!" on page 69.

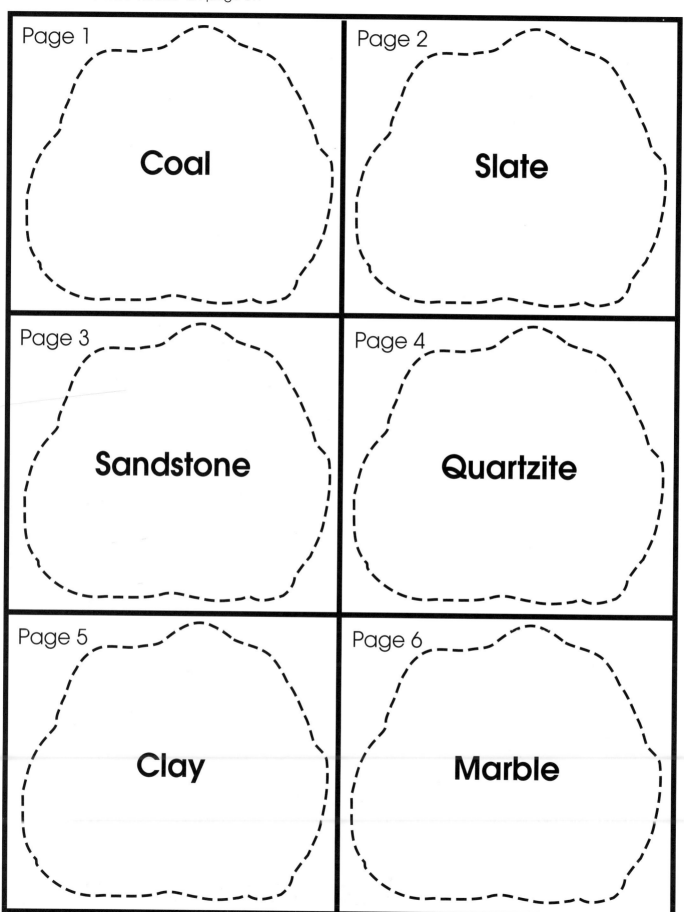

Page 1

Coal

Page 2

Slate

Page 3

Sandstone

Page 4

Quartzite

Page 5

Clay

Page 6

Marble

MARGIE MAGNET

Margie is the main attraction in this magnificent booklet! In advance, gather four 5" x 1" red construction paper strips (for arms and legs), an eight-inch square sheet of aluminum foil, a paper clip, a rubber band, a hairpin, a toothpick, a metal washer, a penny, and a one-inch piece of magnetic tape for each child. Give each student a red construction paper copy of page 78. Also give each student a copy of pages 76–77. (Make enough copies of the booklet page on page 77 for each child to have six.) Have each child cut out the booklet pages and patterns. Help each child cut her sheet of aluminum to fit the backing page and then glue it on as shown. Help her accordion-fold the arms and legs, glue them onto the backing page, and then glue on the hand and feet patterns. Attach the magnetic strip to one hand pattern. Have the child color the cover, sequence the booklet pages, and then staple them onto the backing as shown. Then have her glue the last booklet page onto the backing page. Have her write a page number (2–7) at the bottom of each page. Ask each child to tape one item on each booklet page. Then have her use the magnet to test each item to see whether it is magnetic. Have her answer the question on each page by gluing the correct text box in the space provided. Encourage her to take her booklet home to share her magnetic experience.

EXTENSION ACTIVITY

Have one child pick up paper clips from a table with her hands, while another child picks them up with a magnet. Which way is quicker?

DID YOU KNOW?
- A magnet is an object containing metal that attracts some other metals.
- Natural magnets are in rocks.
- A Greek shepherd named Magnes, who lived about 2,500 years ago, discovered that a certain stone stuck to the iron tip of his shepherd's crook.
- Magnets attract only some kinds of metal, such as iron or steel.

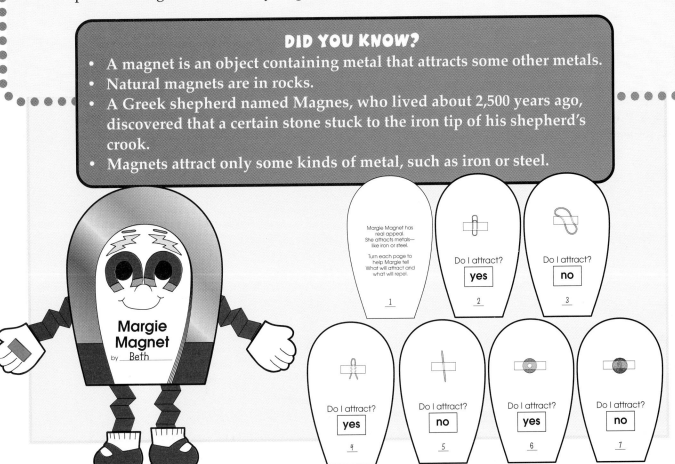

75

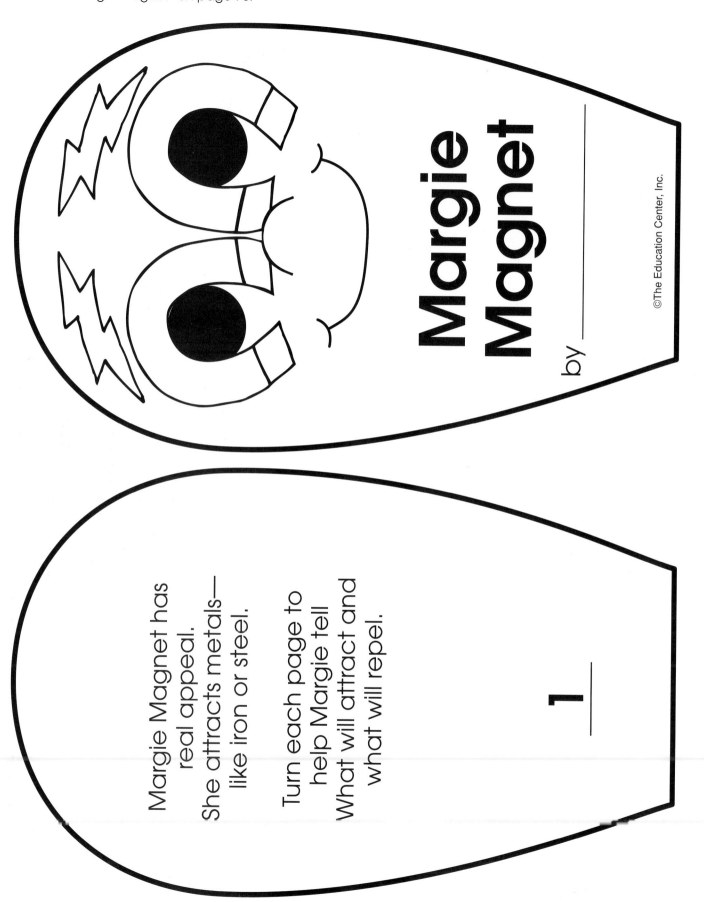

Margie Magnet
by _____

©The Education Center, Inc.

Margie Magnet has
real appeal.
She attracts metals—
like iron or steel.

Turn each page to
help Margie tell
What will attract and
what will repel.

1
___

hands   feet   text boxes

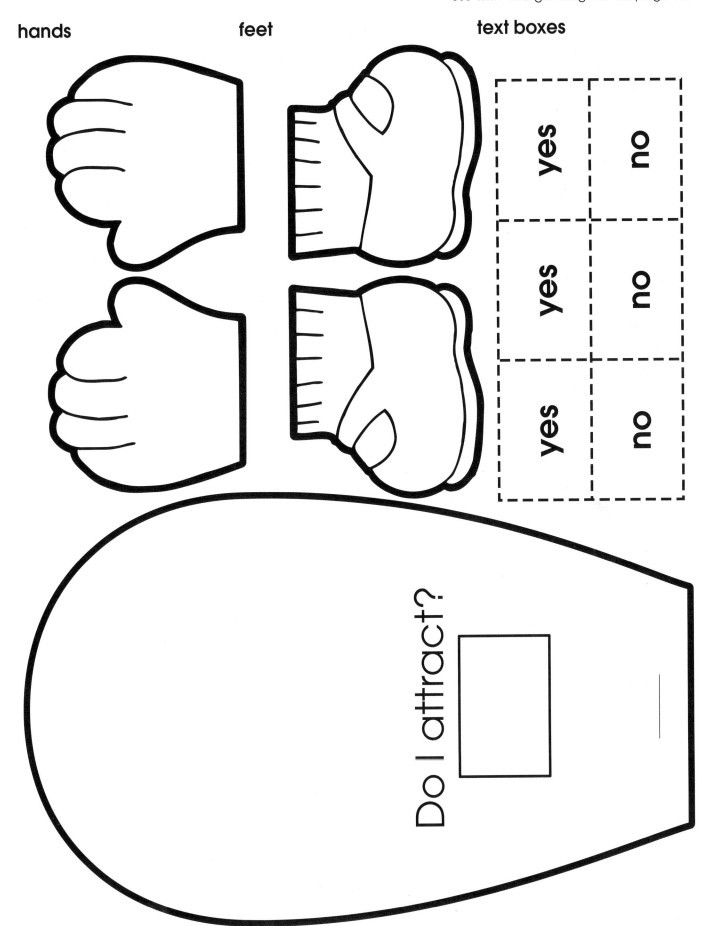

yes	yes	yes
no	no	no

Do I attract?

Booklet Backing Page

Use with "Margie Magnet" on page 75.

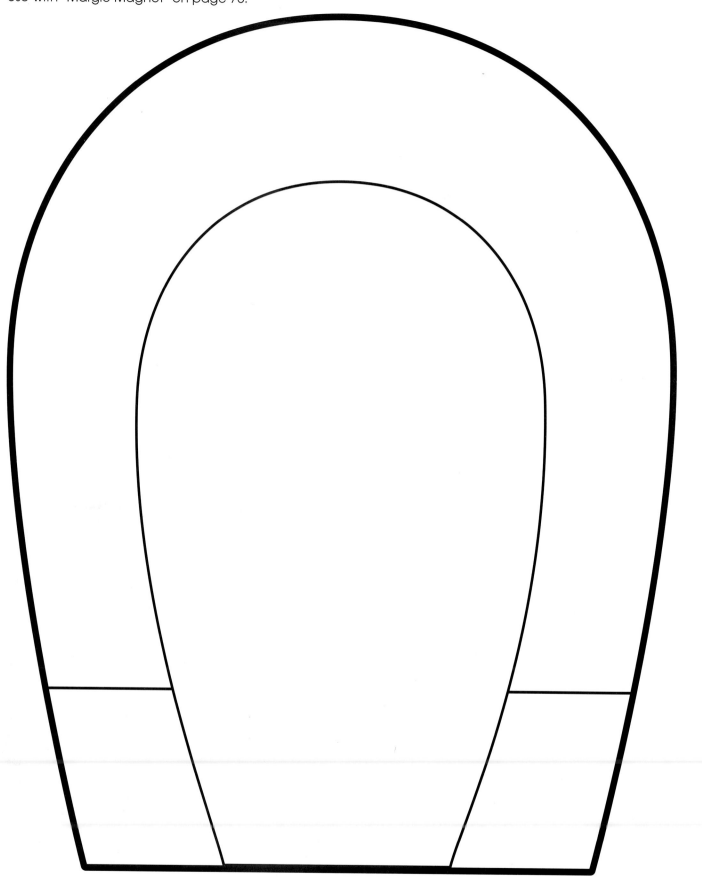

WHAT IS IT?

Youngsters will enjoy following the whale through its environment as they learn about the properties of matter (solid, liquid, and gas). To begin, copy pages 80–83 to make a class supply. Have each child color the whale on each page and then glue a wiggle eye on each one. Have him color each iceberg with a white glitter crayon and then glue the patterns where indicated. Help him paint the water on each page with light blue paint. After the pages have dried, have him sequence the pages behind the cover and staple them together on the left side. Encourage each child to read his booklet and then take it home to share with his family.

EXTENSION ACTIVITY

Play a guessing game of What Is It? with youngsters. Encourage one child at a time to describe something, including whether it is a solid, a liquid, or a gas, for others to try to guess. *(I write with it on the board. It is a solid. What is it? Chalk.)*

DID YOU KNOW?

- Everything on the earth is matter. Matter usually appears as a solid, a liquid, or a gas.
- Solids take up space and have their own shape.
- Liquids take up space and do not have a shape. A liquid takes the shape of its container.
- Gases take up space (as in an inflated balloon), are usually transparent, and do not have a shape. A gas takes the shape of its container.

©The Education Center, Inc.

What Is It?

by

_____

©The Education Center, Inc.

I swim in it.
It is a liquid.
What is it?

1

Water!

2

I swim next to it.
It is a solid.
What is it?

3

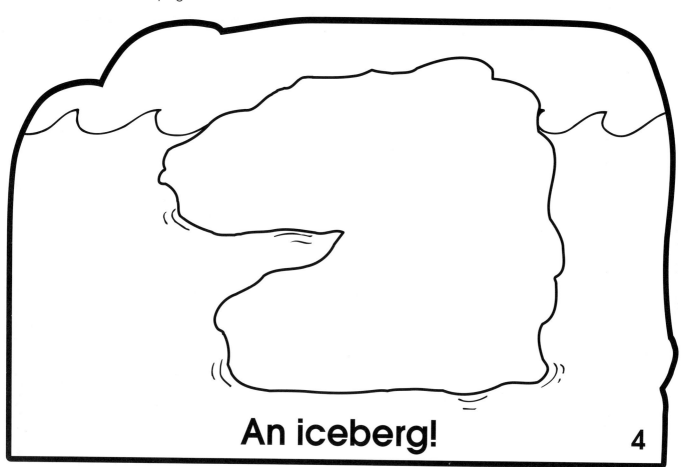

An iceberg!

4

I breathe it.
It is a gas.
What is it?

5

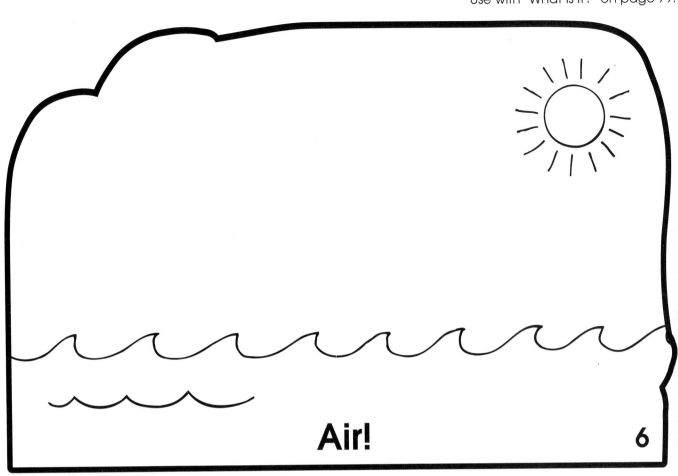

Air! 6

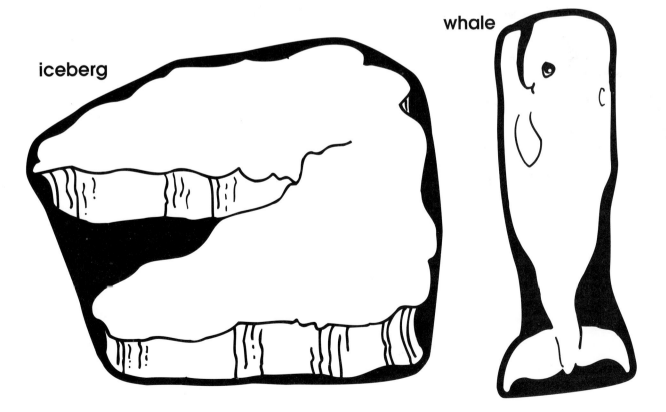

iceberg

whale

FLOATERS AND SINKERS

What do you think—will it sink or will it float like a boat? Have youngsters record their sink and float experiment findings in this fun fold-out booklet. To prepare, collect an apple, a quarter, a leaf, a cork, a marble, and a tub of water. Copy pages 85–88 to make a class supply. Have each child color and cut out her booklet pages and patterns. Help her assemble the booklet by gluing the pages together where indicated. Experiment with one item at a time to determine whether it sinks or floats. Then have each child glue the corresponding pattern on each page either below the water or above the water to designate whether the item sank or floated. Help each child read the text boxes, trace the word *float* or *sink,* and then glue the corresponding sentence in the space provided on each page. When the pages are dry, help her accordion-fold her booklet and then have her read it to a partner. Have each child take her booklet home to share her experiment findings with her family.

EXTENSION ACTIVITY

Have students select more items—such as a pencil, an eraser, and a paper clip—to test as sinkers and floaters. Create a class graph for youngsters to record their findings.

DID YOU KNOW?
- Density is the ratio of the mass of an object compared to its volume.
- The density of an object determines whether it will sink or float.
- Things that float are lighter or less dense than water.
- Things that sink are heavier or more dense than water.

Floaters and Sinkers

by _____ Brad
©The Education Center, Inc.

It will float! 1

It will sink! 2

It will float! 3

It will float! 4

It will sink! 5

Glue page 2 here.

1

Floaters

and

Sinkers

by _____

©The Education Center, Inc.

Booklet Pages
Use with "Floaters and Sinkers" on page 84.

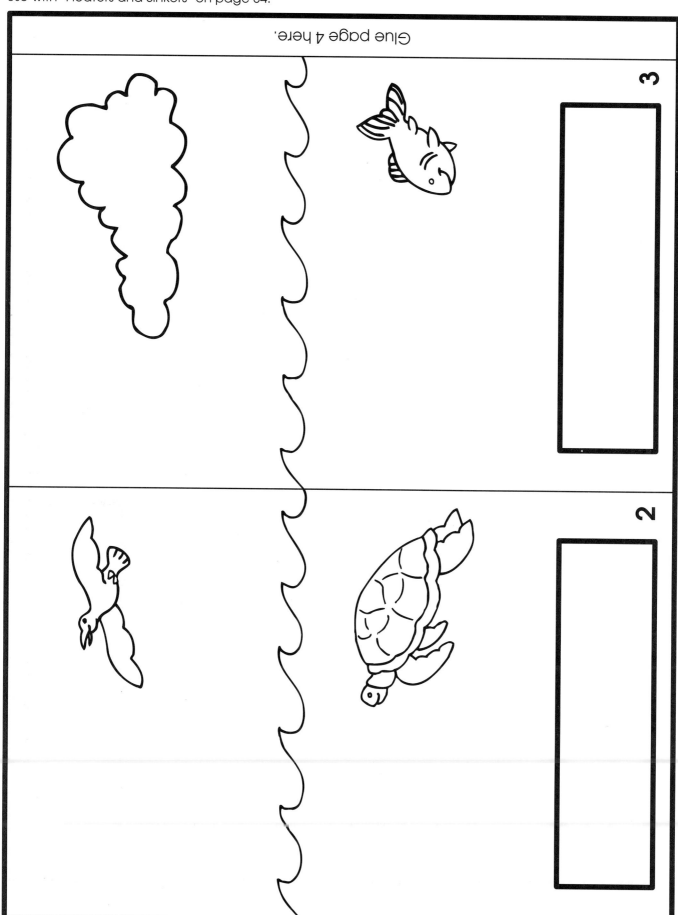

Glue page 4 here.

3

2

5

4

Booklet Patterns and Text Boxes
Use with "Floaters and Sinkers" on page 84.

cork

leaf

marble

apple

quarter

It will float!

It will float! | It will sink!

It will float! | It will sink!

RECYCLE!

Learning to sort and recycle plastic, paper, glass, and metal is easier when youngsters follow the guidance of this classification booklet. Copy pages 90–93 to make a class supply. Have each child color and cut out the booklet pages and patterns. Help him fold back the pocket flap on each page, trace the *L*-shaped line with glue, and then press down the pocket. Have him write his name on the pocket of the cover and then glue the poem on the back side of it as shown. Help him sequence the pages behind the cover and staple them together along the left side. Read all the text to students. Then help each child read his booklet and place the correct pattern in the pocket on each page. Have him store all the patterns in the pocket on the cover and take his booklet home to share his recycling knowledge with family members.

EXTENSION ACTIVITY

Set up a recycling classification center by gathering a variety of plastic containers for youngsters to sort. Ask youngsters to sort into two groups: those that are transparent plastic containers (like clear soda bottles) and those that are opaque plastic containers (like milk jugs).

DID YOU KNOW?

- Recycling saves our natural resources.
- Recycling newspapers into new paper products saves many trees.
- Recycling aluminum cans reduces litter because cans do not decompose.
- Recycling glass reduces the amount of energy it takes to make glass from raw materials.

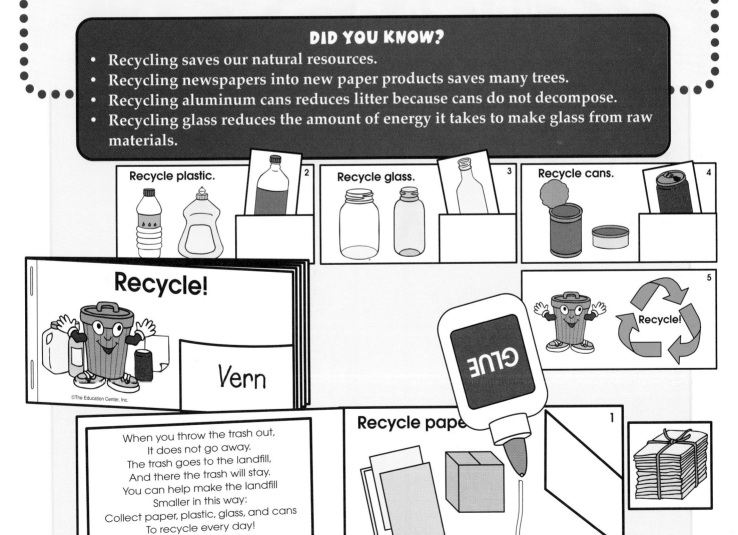

Recycle plastic. 2

Recycle glass. 3

Recycle cans. 4

Recycle! 5

Recycle!

Vern

©The Education Center, Inc.

When you throw the trash out,
It does not go away.
The trash goes to the landfill,
And there the trash will stay.
You can help make the landfill
Smaller in this way:
Collect paper, plastic, glass, and cans
To recycle every day!

Recycle pape

GLUE

1

Booklet Cover and Page

Use with "Recycle!" on page 89.

pocket

pocket

1

Recycle!

Recycle paper.

©The Education Center, Inc.

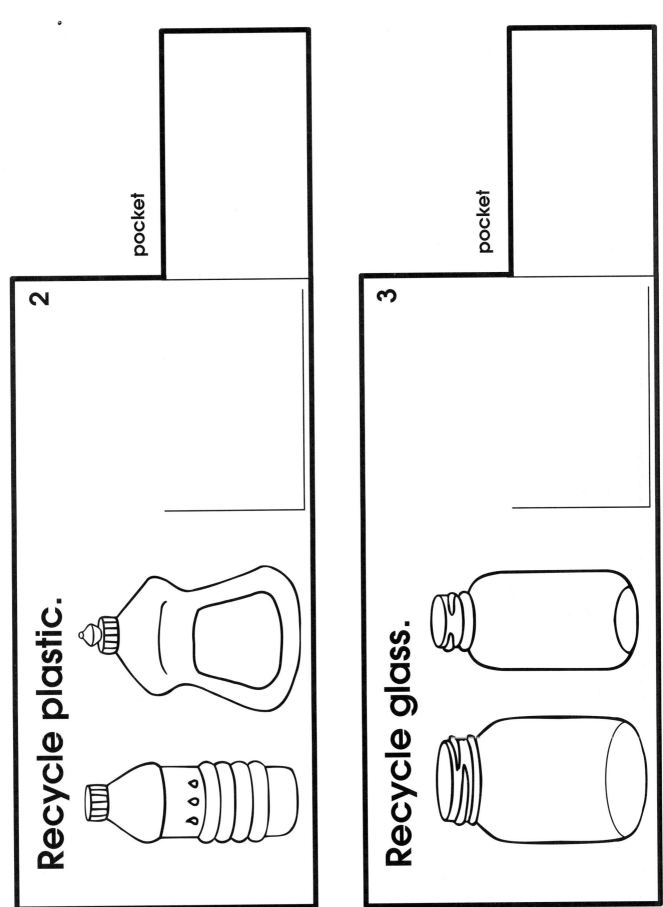

pocket

2

Recycle plastic.

pocket

3

Recycle glass.

4

pocket

Recycle cans.

5

Recycle!

poem

When you throw the trash out,
It does not go away.
The trash goes to the landfill,
And there the trash will stay.
You can help make the landfill
Smaller in this way:
Collect paper, plastic, glass, and cans
To recycle every day!

plastic bottle

glass bottle

aluminum can

newspaper

SPOT'S DAY

Youngsters will love following Spot through his day as he spins through the changing positions of the sun. In advance, copy pages 95–96 to make a class supply. You will also need two nine-inch paper plates and one brad for each child. To prepare, cut out a four-inch pie shape from one plate in each child's set. Ask each child to color and cut out the patterns and text boxes. Have him glue Spot on the right side of the paper plate cutout and glue the title box at the bottom as shown. Glue the other patterns where desired on the plate. Have him glue the wheel pattern (page 95) onto the center of the whole paper plate. Help him glue the corresponding text boxes onto the paper plate above the appropriate sun or moon illustration as shown. Then help him attach the two paper plates with a brad as shown. Encourage each child to read section 1 and then spin the bottom plate to read the rest of the story.

EXTENSION ACTIVITY

Have each child create a chart of the positions of the sun at home. Fold a sheet of paper into four sections and then label the sections "morning," "lunch," "dinner," and "night." Ask the child to draw a picture of the sun or moon and an appropriate activity for each section. Then have each child return his chart to share at school.

DID YOU KNOW?

- The moon moves around the earth in an orbit.
- The earth moves around the sun in an orbit.
- The sun is the closest star to the earth.
- It takes 24 hours, or one day, for the sun to pass directly overhead and return to the same position.

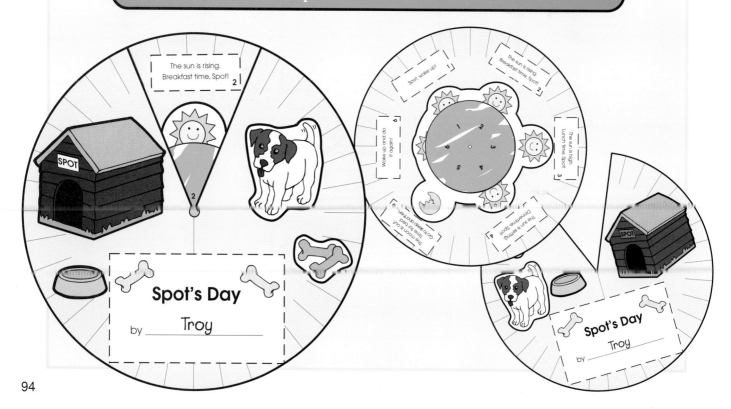

Spot's Day

by _____

©The Education Center, Inc.

Spot

Spot, wake up!

1

The sun is rising.
Breakfast time, Spot!

2

The sun is high.
Lunchtime, Spot!

3

The sun is setting.
Dinnertime, Spot!

4

The moon is out.
Time for bed.
Go to sleep and then... 5

Wake up and do
it again!

6

SPOT